The World You See

Change the World You See One Person at a Time! Starting with you!

By

Christine Chandler

Published 2021 by Christine Chandler

YOUMEANDTHEWORLDYOUSEE.COM

Edited by Braelyn DeRocher

Disclaimer

This book is dedicated to:

I would like to dedicate this book to my children Eric, Marissa, Madalyn and Lucas. I hope that one day they will learn that with faith and trust in the universe that anything is possible. That everything starts with a dream. I hope that through my journey they can find their way along their path. Learning that loving themselves first is the best investment that they can ever make. I hope this book teaches you that you must follow your path. The path that is right for you. I will never judge you or love you any less. I am grateful to be a part of the lessons you are here to learn.

Table of Contents

Preface

I start all my writings by setting an intention. I call upon the Universe and ask for assistance while writing this book. I ask that the book provides a message of the highest quality. Allowing it to act as a catalyst for those that read it. Influencing them to allow their passions to lead. Knowing that with faith and a dream anything is possible. That they have the ability to influence the world they live in through love. My will, Thy will, Divine will.

Introduction

As I write this book I am not worried about if it is successful--all I know is that I have the urge to write it. I trust that no matter what happens, whether it is a redirection or it is an undoing, the universe has my back. As you get further into the book, I will discuss with you the importance of your words and writing a manifesto. Writing this book was part of my manifesto, a part of my ever growing spiritual journey. Part of my journey was to set an intention of helping others that are like myself. One thing that I hope you take away from this book is the importance of loving yourself and the role it plays in shaping the world you see. I would like to think of this book as the conversation between you and me about, "The World You See!"

Just know through this journey everyone awakens differently. Some people are born with the knowledge of what they have come here to do, while others have many lessons to learn throughout their lives. There will be individuals that will experience some very traumatic events that will then cause them to be thrown into their awakening shaking up their whole world. There is a huge misconception that awakenings are all rainbows and butterflies and I would be doing you a real in-justice if I led you to believe that the spiritual path is easy. Your journey (or spiritual awakening) will however, be the most fulfilling path you will take. Awakenings do teach us what is really important in our lives.

It has been my experience that many question their worthiness, their sanity, personal belief systems and find that their whole lives are turned upside down. I personally had so many questions and spent a great deal of time searching for answers. Only to find that I would constantly be led back to focus on myself. At times I felt as though I was crazy and alone. I am here to tell you that you are not alone, nor are you crazy. There are many others like you experiencing or have experienced something similar. The important thing to remember is that the spiritual journey is about growing your soul. There will be times that are easy and go smoothly; there will also be times you will be met with obstacles. Some obstacles will be easy to maneuver through, as others will be difficult. There will be times you feel empowered and other times you will feel alone, but in the end, I can assure you that you will feel whole. You will begin to wonder how you ever lived your life without the knowledge that you will gain through discovery of self and source.

As you may feel in your spiritual journey that you want answers right away, I too felt the same way. I wanted to know the five W's (who, what, when, where, and why) and I wanted to know who before me had these similar experiences. What started one's awakening and when did they experience it in their lifetime? Where did they find guidance and knowledge? Everything that I once believed and knew to be true of myself was being questioned. Everything that I had worked so hard to do and be over my lifetime to that point was in question. I felt like I was living a life that was a lie. I always knew that there was something more in this world--something that was far greater than I could ever imagine. Deep down there was something that I was always searching for because it was missing.

The truth is, the W's do not matter. The fact of the matter is, you are currently in the now. The reason you are here no longer matters, the past no longer exists and the future is yet to arrive. You only have this moment, right now in this moment you know your life is changing or you have to make a change in your life. Understanding that the way you once did things may no longer work for you.

I hope that this book provides you guidance, clarity and inspiration to bring your awareness back to self.
Reminding you how important the role you play in your life is and how it truly impacts the world you see.

I want you to ask yourself these questions before you go any further.

1: If we were sitting on the moon together looking down at the earth, what would your world look like to you?

2: Would you be proud of what you see, or would you want to change it?

I was asked these questions. When I was compiling my answer, I wanted to be logical and politically correct. Then a light bulb went off in my head. The answer was so much simpler.

Answer to Question 1: Love! Love is the answer. Love for everyone regardless of race, religion, gender, sexual orientation, political views etc. Love for people just as they are--this includes us. If we cannot love ourselves humanity doesn't stand a chance.

Answer to Question 2: At first my answer was no; I would not have been proud of what I saw. Look what the world is going through, a pandemic, riots, a fallen economy, hate, you name it the world is going through it.

If you asked me now, I would tell you I do not need to be proud of how the world is, but what I can do in the now to allow my light to shine in it.

My advice is that you meditate, pray, whatever you do that helps you find guidance and ask them for a sign. What can you do to help shine a light back on humanity? If you do not get an answer right away, it is ok. Right now, in this moment, you can do one thing and that is focus on yourself because love/self-love is the answer.

That is right, it all starts with YOU! The only way that we can get back to humanity is self- love. Although, right now you may think that you are such a small part of humanity, learning to love yourself has the largest impact. How you love yourself is how you love others. Not only must we love the good parts of ourselves we let everyone see we must also love the parts of ourselves we lock away in the deepest parts of our being. Only then can you experience the true meaning of unconditional love and acceptance. Once you can love yourself unconditionally, loving others for who they are is easy.

How I Got Here

You are probably asking yourself, how did she start her journey?

Well, to be honest for me there was no other option. The Universe made it clear that it was something I had to embrace. My spiritual awakening sent me into a state of confusion and the world of Christine Chandler was in a place of total chaos. In the beginning, there was so much change going on in my life all at one time. This life I had built was changing so fast and I was trying to control it. My finances were up in the air, my marriage was a mess, my heart was broken and the job I loved so much was just not as fulfilling as it used to be. I had spent a decade plus working and building a life, doing things that we are brought up to believe are going to bring us to living a full life--well, at least that's what I was taught. Work hard, do more, get more, have more and be more that were the common themes. Yet, after I would achieve what I worked for it would be onto the next. Never really taking time to enjoy the fruits of my labor and as a result, it left me empty. I was empty in a lot of ways but had more than most, so I was ok with it. Something was still missing and I went looking for it. I looked for it through people, things and places but never in the one place that really mattered. I didn't even stop to look at myself. What was I doing that was impacting the world I see and how I perceive it? If this chaos is happening in my life, how am I projecting this chaos onto others?

One thing that never even crossed my mind is that I was setting myself up for heartbreak. There were things that I was doing that were shaping the world around me as I knew it. The crazy thing was I was stuck in the mindset of pointing fingers and blaming others. Not taking responsibility for how I was allowing things to happen in my life because the universe is going to give you what you believe you deserve. The universe was going to send back to me exactly what I was giving to myself and others; I did not believe I was deserving of love--I did not believe it; I certainly did not think I was receiving it, at least not what I expected love to be. Since I did not believe I deserved love in the past, I never allowed anyone to really love me or get close to me. Maybe I was setting my expectations too high? Maybe my expectations of how things were supposed to happen were hindering me from seeing the full picture? There is much more to say about my own thought process and how it impacted the way I looked at the world around me. I would be here all day typing and let us just save a little for a later discussion. Right now, I am just going to focus on how I discovered that I was not giving myself the love that I wanted so much from others.

It was time! It was time for change! No one could change the world around me but, me! It all started with me, therefore, I had to be the start of the change. I was already reading so I decided to read more. A few of the books I read were, *Are You an Earth Angel* by Tanya Carrol Richardson, *The Power of Now* by Ekhart Tolle, *The Complete Reader* by Neville Goddard. I was reading so many books to find answers that I finally just subscribed to Kindle Unlimited through amazon. In my reading I noticed a common theme throughout each book was loving yourself to unlock the world around you. This was not just loving the things about myself I liked, it had to be the things I disliked, too. There were tears, laughs and outbursts, just to name a few things. In hindsight I understand it all. I started really looking at myself. What were things I liked about me? What were things I disliked about me? What were things I was grateful for in my life? What were things I wanted to change? I needed a new perspective. I started doing one thing every day to show myself that, I LOVED ME! I started naming things I was grateful for every day. I was working out and eating better, I never missed a Monday, I was reading blogs and learning about being mindful and I began journaling. Through this journey, I rediscovered my intuition while all along, it was inside of me. I was just so closed off I could not hear it. Things were changing, I was changing. I was starting to really love myself-- ALL of me, even the things I carried guilt, shame and judgement for. The world as I saw it was changing. Everything I once knew was now something for me to reflect on.

Through my healing process the world around me was healing, too. As I let my light shine, the people around me were also starting to change. Through my journaling I was beginning to accept myself for who I was and the things that made me who I am. Through showing myself compassion I began to see I was able to have more compassion for others. In the past where I had difficulty with empathy, it was now becoming so much easier. Changing the way I was operating I was able to see that people just want to be accepted for who they are at the moment that you meet them.

Unfortunately, I had to get to a place where I felt like I was losing everything before I even realized that I had to start loving myself. I had to stop expecting others to carry me emotionally. I was not a soul having an emotional experience and I was living my emotions. The reality was I still had everything I needed, but my perception needed to change. However, my perception was not changing, my perception was my reality. Much of what I was experiencing was controlled by the narrative I was telling myself. I was so focused on what others were doing and not doing for me to show me they loved me, that I failed to look at the one person that could change it all... ME! Let me make this clear, it was not easy. I decided I wanted to get back to the basics, I wanted to do something that I enjoyed. I wanted something that I could be consistent and persistent with so I did not feel like I was failing myself. I started reading; I continued to go to the gym; I started eating better and I started feeling better. Life around me before you knew it, became brighter, less overwhelming and full of positive vibrations.

I felt like the universe had turned its back on me. The hardest reality I had to face was the universe did not turn its back on me, but I had turned my back on myself. After a lot of time sitting alone with my thoughts, I decided the best approach for self-discovery was to address each question one at a time. No matter how well laid out the plan you have in your mind is, it never truly goes as intended. My journey of self-discovery really did not allow for answers to come one at a time, it was more like following a trail of breadcrumbs allowing for self-discovery along the way.

We all hope to have some impact and make a difference in the world in some way. The realization came to mind that to have any chance of influencing any type of change, I must be the change I wanted to see. For me, I really began to focus on: What if I just looked at myself through the lenses in which I see the world, what would I see? Would I be proud of what I saw? Would I want to change myself? How would I change myself? Could I make a difference? I needed to change my perspective. Changing humanity has too many external factors that I can't control. The one thing I could control is how I look at myself and my patterns of thinking. That is where I really started to dive deep into who Christine Chandler is. What is her divine purpose?

As I dove into my journey, I started with developing a routine. I found the routine was important because, on the not so great days we tend to revert back to our habits. The most important thing that I do daily is remind myself that I have the power to choose how to approach things. This allows for flexibility. After all, we never really know what the day has in store for us and the only thing we can control is how we respond. When I need to be brought back to the present moment, I will name things that I am grateful for. I sit in the presence of never forgetting to do one thing daily that is designated just for me-- I call this, showing yourself some love. This can be as simple as sitting and looking up at the sky because you find it beautiful and it is what you want to do. Showing yourself some love is much more than telling yourself I love you. It is the combinations of the words and actions that matter. Let me ask you if you told yourself I love you and never put action behind it would you believe those words? How about if you went and spent time with yourself doing something that brings you joy? Then would you believe that you were showing yourself love? Sometimes it is not the words that we hear, but the actions we are taking. One thing I learned was how love is shown in many forms. It can be as easy as setting time aside for yourself to do some self-care. Some self-care practices I do are styling my hair, applying make-up, taking a bubble bath and I set at least 15 minutes a day for meditation. During my times of self-care, I continue to make a conscious effort to talk to myself with kindness and compassion. I truly start and end my day with positive affirmations.

When I found this internal unkindness within myself, I started setting boundaries with not only myself, but others as well. Creating boundaries with myself gave me the time to focus on journaling which helped me listen to my intuition and identify what I was passionate about such as singing and writing this book for my followers. The more I went internal, the more learning there needed to be and that is why I started taking classes to fine tune my intuition.

Everyone on Earth has the ability to work with their intuition. Will it be easy? No, but I promise it will be worth it! Through this process of self-discovery you will cry, you will laugh, but you will heal. In this healing process you will find comfort, compassion, self-acceptance, forgiveness and most importantly an understanding of who you are. Internally, you have always felt like something was missing inside of you, this much I know. I encourage you to take it one day at a time.

Cultivating your soul will lead you to remember what you value the most. It will reopen a flood gate of memories leading you back to your purpose in this lifetime. The purpose of finding love, (Love of yourself, love of others, love for life) finding love in being by positive energy into yourself and your passion. As you do so you will discover new things about you, your passions, people and the world around you. If you feel like you can go one more day, then give me another day.

The important thing to remember is that living out of a place of love is your choice. It is your birthright to feel love and love the divine being that you are. Through your healing you will find that you will begin to heal the people around you. The love you will find for yourself you will put out into the world and that love will find its way back into your life. What you put out, you get back! Your healing will even be a starting point for other people that you will never meet. We are all connected, we all are here to help each other. It is time to let your light out! It is time for your heart to shine! It is your turn!

This is the moment--the moment that you take the first step down the path on your journey. Trust in the process because every moment of your life has led you to this moment. The moment where you choose to discover the purpose for your life, spoiler alert, your life is your purpose! How you choose to live your purpose is the question. Are you going to continue to live with the belief that things happen to you or things happen for you? Remember everything is perspective. In order to claim the abundant life you have always dreamed of, you must change your perspective.

Decide today that you are going to choose yourself and chase your dreams. Your past does not have to define you.

Yes, this may mean that people will leave your life but, that does not mean they are gone forever--it may just mean right now. What is meant for you will always be yours. Even if it is just for a moment, it was still yours and no one can ever take that away. The only limiting thing in your life are the thoughts and beliefs that you hold inside. Consider your mind the prison and your thoughts are the warden. The Universe wants you to know that changing the way you view the world around you is not an easy process. However, it is without a doubt fulfilling in the end. Remember it is the mind that tells us no. and the Universe always says, YES!

Your heart is leading you where you need to go. The need to control and follow logic is what you have been conditioned to do in the past. You are not meant to be the past version of yourself--trust your heart; trust your intuition. The brain has a way of wanting to make the simplest answers difficult and the brain is a tool that in the past you have allowed to control and make sense of things to give them meaning or purpose. This does not have to be so hard, this answer that you are looking for is so simple. Love, love is the answer! Invest in loving yourself; Invest in the things that bring love in your life; Invest in the things that bring the joy back to your journey. By investing in yourself, you will continue to see that even when faced with difficult times you will find they will pass quicker.

The number one investment that you can ever make when it comes to your highest good is to invest in yourself now. Yes, there will be times that you need to glance into the future or look to the past. However, at this very moment, the most important investment is to invest into yourself and feed your soul. This investment is going to have the utmost impact on your future.

Do not waste your time worrying if you are making it up. Remember that you must have faith in where you are being led. There is a reason and purpose for it all, within this you will see that purpose soon. You need to trust in divine timing. Right now, focus on keeping yourself in the higher vibrations as much as possible. If you have to tell yourself, "I choose to focus on me! My journey is my journey! No one else can do it for me"!

Your Purpose

The one thing that is important to remember is the spiritual journey is a journey inward. Before you can ever really understand the role that you are playing in life and your connection to the universe you must first really discover yourself. Who are you? What is it that you value? What is it that you want? What brings you to a place of happiness and joy? How do you see yourself living your best life? These are all hard questions to answer.

If you have lived a life pleasing others. For far too long you and others like you have put the needs of others first, allowing your own needs and desires to be suppressed. When this happens you lose your identity. Always giving your energy allows others to be lifted. There is absolutely NOTHING wrong with you taking your life back, standing up for what you believe in and setting strong boundaries while chasing your dreams.

You may lose some people along the way, but do not worry because you will never be alone. Many of us have been programmed to put the needs of others before our own. In doing so, our own needs and desires have become just a distant memory. It is about identifying what you value most and growing your soul. It will reopen a flood gate of memories leading you back to your purpose in this lifetime. The purpose of finding love

16

is to love yourself, love others, love for life and finding love in being. Find love in creating by putting positive energy into yourself and your passion. As you do so you will discover new things about you, your passions, people and the world around you. Learning to trust in faith, the power of your mind and power of the, "I AM" one step at a time. You will come to a place where you become confident and find excitement in the knowing that you can overcome and create the life you desired all along.

In order to find your life's purpose, you must first look at your life. I want you to take a step back and look around you, look at your situation, look at where you have come from and most importantly look internally. You are the key to understanding your purpose because inside you are all the keys to unlocking this purpose. The thing you really need to know right now is that you are exactly where you need to be. Everything that you have done, your family has done, people around you have done have led you right to this moment. There are moments that you are not even aware of that have brought you right here. The short answer is, YES, you have a purpose.

Never doubt you have a purpose in this lifetime, but know this, you cannot see the finish line so be in the moment. Every person that you encounter has a potential message for you to learn so, make sure you are paying attention. As you walk through life and new people enter your space, know they, too, deserve to be seen. See them, know they are there. There are many lessons these individuals will teach you such as things that do not serve you, sadly through the pain there is growth. What if the ones that teach you about pain are the ones that loved you the most but just could not love themselves? In these times, remember to show compassion, love and acceptance. Forgive yourself when you feel that you are being judgmental, it just means you are seeing something in you that brings out emotion, just make sure you identify those emotions. Identifying the emotions will provide you the tools to navigate this world more freely. It will allow you to clear your mind and see things as they really are.

We are all souls here having a human experience. Everyone is here to learn their lessons, master them and manifest their hearts desires. What one person wants, and desires may not be the same for another. This is key when we are observing others. We must not judge or envy the life they have because we do not know the lessons they have learned along the way.

One thing that many forget is that being human is experiencing emotion. Love, joy, happiness, sadness, and anger are a few examples. Once a soul understands that they are experiencing their emotions and not embodying their emotions, the experience becomes more manageable. Everyone's soul at some point or another will experience something that does not bring them joy. The goal is to find a way to be grateful for the experience. How they react to it is key to their experience. Not every experience will be positive or negative; some experiences will just be an experience, something that one will carry with them and refer to at some point in their lifetime. Even the most positive people have days where thoughts can lead them astray.

Once a soul identifies that it is their thoughts and internal conversation with themselves that construct the experiences they receive in their external world, it is then when they become very mindful with their thoughts. There are many that will never be awakened to that idea during their lifetime. These souls will then become victims of their circumstances and their external environment. Remember that there are some that only see the bad broken parts of the world.

Another important lesson that I learned was there is no right and wrong. There is no right way or perfect science to any of this. What works for one person may not work for you. Allow curiosity to lead the way and do not be afraid to try and learn different things. The experiences will help you identify what is right for you and what is not-- it comes down to faith and belief. That is why it is important for you to know what it is you value? What is it you believe? What is it that can become a practice for you?

How you walk in knowing is up to you. The only true right or wrong would be where your mind says is right and wrong--no one else can determine that for you. That would mean you were allowing the values and beliefs of others to influence how you navigate your spirituality.

Spirituality is a personal journey. It is a journey or knowing your soul and realization that you are one with the universe. Learning and developing your own ways of manifesting the life you desire and living your most authentic life--not the life determined by others. Allowing your mind and your desires to work with the universe as one. As you begin to follow and trust in the universe, the universe will continue to open new paths. Those paths help us align with our desires and that special thing inside us. We all have something special to give the world. How you decide to allow it to be seen and given is totally up to you.

Living your most authentic life is part of your purpose. Accepting yourself and others for who they are in the moment that you meet them. Knowing that you have no control over what they do and how they think. The only thing that any soul has control over is how they react to situations and the manifestations that they attract during their lifetime. We are all here to learn that we are the great, "I AM" working simultaneously with the universe to create the life we imagine. Every situation in your life has manifested from a thought that started in your imagination. How your life plays out from there is determined by the choices you make in the present moment.

Even the souls that seem to go with the flow all have a vision of some type. An idea of where they want their life to go. For some people the process comes more freely than others. There are many that must overcome emotional traumas due to environments or circumstances that they were raised in. Trauma does not make people any less capable of manifesting an abundant life, it is just part of one's journey and the lessons they chose to learn here on earth. Ideally, manifesting is the integration of the lessons and skills that one learns. As a person learns one lesson and they continue to raise or in some cases lower their vibrational frequency they will find that new cycles and new lessons will be presented.

Once a soul begins to become aware that they can influence their manifestations through their thoughts and emotions it is beneficial for them to develop a vision. To develop a vision, one first must identify what they are learning and what skills they currently have that can assist them with this. They must then identify their truth and once a soul can identify their truth in the moment it is key to seek guidance from the universe. This is done by turning inward through mediation or seeking answers through spiritual teachers. Ultimately, all the answers you seek are already inside you because it requires you to work with the subconscious. This will assist in clarifying what you want to incorporate or seek in your vision. Working with the subconscious allows you to look at what you do and do not want to allow you to release what does not serve you. Then providing an opportunity for you to replace it with things that will serve your highest good. Your soul will lead you where it is meant to go. Yes, sometimes you will be led to some hard lessons, but they will always be for your highest good even when you cannot see.

Earlier, I discussed how your life is your purpose. This is where I really get to explain exactly what that means. Remember, we are all here having a human experience and each one of us experiences life and its challenges. We all are here to learn, how we learn manifests through experiences, relationships and places we interact throughout the course of our life. Through this journey, everyone's path is individualized by their divine truth and soul contract. How I do life may not be how you or someone else decide to do life. We are all met with some type of adversity during our lifetime and these adversities can often be looked at as misfortunes. I want you to look back at your life and ask yourself the following questions (maybe write them down and answer them yourself-- let your words flow onto the paper): What are some significant events that may have been challenging that you had to overcome? What did you learn from them? If you had to relive the same situation all over again today, would you make the same decisions or would you choose a different path based on what you learned earlier?

If you would have asked me 5 years ago how adversities impacted my life, I would have looked at you and said what in the world are you talking about? I just considered them events that I had no choice but to either let make or break me. Breaking me was never an option because I had something to prove.

I had to prove that no matter what, I could do more. I would not end up the failure that others expected because I had a kid at a young age, or chose a path someone did not approve of. It did not see them as moments that would bring me wisdom or that would help me reach people and be relatable. I just saw it as I was chasing a goal and in order to reach the goal, I had to overcome whatever was thrown my way.

Now when challenges are thrown at me, I identify adversities as challenges presented to me that I must navigate. I challenge you to look at your life and identify those adversities in your life yourself. While you think of these adversities, you may realize that they have either brought life changing decisions that may or may not have been beneficial. However, responding to adversity is key because some will respond with grace and ease, while others may become overwhelmed.

The trials and adversities that we experience in our lives teach us many things. In some cases, they will teach us to re-evaluate very traumatic events and then become a guide to help others overcome similar events that may even present itself in our future. Others will teach us to stand up for the things we believe in while teaching us how to not back down and have unwavering faith in ourselves to overcome obstacles. On the contrary, not all adversity lessons are negative, sometimes they teach us compassion and empathy in order to understand the world around us.

With this, the obstacles we face and experience in our life journey helps allow us to bring wisdom and guidance to the world. As we grow into our new found self and skills, it provides us with new perspectives aided by kindness that helps us interact and change the world. Being able to understand ourselves and others makes it easier for us to relate and navigate obstacles in some shape or form and make what we are able to give the world a very special place. Without human experience, there would be no adversity and everyone around us would see things the same way, which would not allow for human or spiritual growth. They can have similar experiences, but they will never be the same. Without adversity, there would only be one way of seeing things: there would be no human growth.

Like many people, I was once a believer that my life was what it was. My life seemed as though I had a laundry list of obstacles that I had to react to or overcome for a long period of time. Granted, I always had a semi-positive outlook on life does not mean that I was always outwardly optimistic. As I write this book, I often find myself saying, "I wish I would have been led to this information 20 years ago." My life would have been so different. However, I would not be the person I have become without the experiences I had. Then I must remind myself to be grateful for things happening the way they did. Regardless, of how or why there was good that came with any bad that was experienced. As I began to find gratitude in the experience, I started to see the good outweigh the bad significantly.

Accepting Change

As hard as it may be, it is vital that you accept that things are constantly changing, things grow and things die because life is all about movement. Life is like the seasons we experience. Spring comes and life blossoms over the summer and then fall comes and we shake the leaves off the trees in preparation for the sleep of winter. The change of the seasons brings us back to something new to be birthed next spring. If one resists these changes, our souls experience regression and halts our healing growth and learning. Taking you through this journey, my hope is to guide you away from the idea that change is terrifying and provide you with some insight that change is in fact a beautiful experience. In the book, *The Power of Now Ekhart Tolle* states, "Some changes look negative on the surface, but you will soon realize that space is being created for something new to emerge." This quote means that, even the most unwanted change can open space for the most fulfilling moments in a lifetime, there is always a lesson to be learned through experiencing a change of any kind.

There will be days that going with the flow and embracing change will come easily. On the other hand, there will be days old thought patterns that somehow begin to find their way to the surface. Ask yourself, what are the thoughts that keep you in a place of fear? What are the thoughts that are hindering your ability to see the

25

good that is happening in your life? Yes, there may be things not going great but I can assure you there is good to be found. These are thoughts that want to suck you back into thinking that you are not worthy, things will not get better, or you are not good enough.

I am here to tell you that you are more than enough and you are worthy. I know you may not be able to see it right now, but you must stop resisting change that the universe gives to you. You must stop trying to control the outcomes because resisting will only bring more obstacles. Do not hold back your emotions because you are afraid of being vulnerable. Vulnerability is a strength and continuing to change your thought patterns will allow you to lean on your vulnerabilities, turning them into tools you will use when met with future challenges. The universe will always guide you down the right path to your divine calling because divine timing is everything. Things may not make a lot of sense right now, but you will see when the time is right. It is time for you to believe and trust that the changes that are happening are for your highest good. By speaking the positivity into your life, you will find that you are met with more positive experiences. Trust me when I tell you this, the more you speak positivity internally the easier life will become.

There will constantly be times that moments of doubt will surface. In times of self-doubt, you need to continue to practice replacing those doubts with thoughts that serve you. Believing that you have all the tools you need

26

to move forward in such a way that aligns for outcomes that are favorable for all. Soon you will see that those moments of doubt will not come as often. I know that there have been times where those moments would last what felt like lifetimes and is essential to be consistent and persistent. Remember, you are a soul having a human experience. Part of that human experience is feeling all emotions to include doubt. In those times feel it, identify the trigger and release it. One must acknowledge emotional feelings when they arise; if you are feeling angry, say it; if you are feeling sad, write down why. You must write down why certain things make you feel a certain way to get to the root cause of the issue. It is important to express, not repress it. When we repress emotion it manifests in other ways. Some ways repressed emotions have been known to manifest is through physical pain and troubled relationships. Use that energy in a positive way. There are many avenues to creative outlets to turn these negative emotions into positive energies. Do you like to paint, sing, garden, go for a walk, anything that brings you joy will work. You must allow yourself to adjust and feel the flow of your emotions by placing yourself in the now. The feeling of emotions is part of the human experience. While manifesting the life you desire, you need to allow yourself to detach from the outcome, releasing the worry because worry is a wasted emotion pulling you away from opportunities that are presented in the now.

Be grateful for the little wins because the little wins bring hope, light and guidance to your divine path during the changes you encounter and embrace them in bliss while releasing doubt. As I will continually repeat, change is hard, but it is necessary. Life is an exchange of endless changes and this will continue with or without you, it is up to you to decide if you interact positively with these changes. The positive thing about change is that it means you have an opportunity every day to make new choices-- an opportunity to be reborn. Yes, you may have some of the same problems, but you get to face those problems differently if you so choose to. That means who you were yesterday is not who you are not today.

Do not get lost in the idea of being stuck, feeling unworthy or whatever self-imposed belief you have bestowed upon yourself. Do not resist the changes happening in your life because the more you try to hold on to where you are, the more resistance you are going to experience -- life is constantly changing, which means nothing stays the same. How do you embrace that change when it seems to be one event after another?

Here are a few ways that you can embrace change:

1. Love yourself first
2. Clear out your environment (decluttering allows for new things to be received)
3. Go with the flow
4. rediscover amusement (doing things that bring you joy)
5. Do not judge (we are all experiencing our own lessons in different ways)
6. Stay true to your faith
7. Trust that things are happening for your highest good
8. Believe that things are happening for you
9. Find the good in the situation
   Release expectation of how things are supposed to go
10. Find a way to get excited
11. Know that change brings in new
12. Put good energy into things you find joy in
13. Find a way to be of service
14. Show interest in others
15. Acceptance
16. Consider it a new adventure

Change from the universe is important because it is clearing out aspects of your life that are keeping internal and external energy from evolving. Let us start making decisions, taking the leap into the unknown and allow the universe to lead the way. Knowing that ultimately, we only have control over how we react to the changes that are happening. If you throw all caution to the wind and start welcoming this "roller coaster" in life, while knowing that there will be good in every day, you will become more aware of these guided moments.

Power of Choice

We as humans want instant gratification but these changes do not happen overnight. My advice to you would be to release all expectations on how you think things will happen and not put a time frame on the things in which you manifested. Life is like planting a garden, when you plant a garden there is preparation that needs to be done before you harvest. Investing time into a garden you must till the soil, plant the seeds, water, weed and feed--the same applies to your soul growth. It is not like one day you wake up and you do not have to deal with your daily life, in fact, it is quite the opposite.

There was one major theme that I learned through all my reading, learning and personal experience. I learned that it is vital to understand your mind and the ability to manifest your thoughts into your reality. Everything a person experiences is due to thoughts they give power to. Projection, learned behavior, addiction and codependency are some examples in which negative thoughts may impact your surroundings. When I do readings or live events, some questions shine light on the negative thought patterns that may endure. Some of these questions are: "Why am I attracted to a particular type of situation?" or, "Will I ever find someone that really loves me"? When I am talking, coaching and giving guidance from spirit the message, I often find being delivered is to pay attention to the dialog you have with yourself daily. The only way you will ever attract a different situation is when you start to approach things inside you differently. Really taking a deep look at how you talk and interact with yourself will show you exactly what you've essentially manifested into your life. When you start to change the interaction within, you will begin to see that the situations you find yourself in begin to change also. In, *The Complete Reader* by Neville Goddard he states, "Man attracts what he is." What this statement is referring to is that a person will attract things that are in alignment with what they believe true of themselves. If you believe yourself to be unworthy of being loved, then you will attract relationships that lack love. The ideas and belief that you hold true regardless if they are just a thought or spoken word is the energy that radiates out.

It is important to be mindful of where you allow your thoughts to take you. Remember, your thoughts quickly manifest into the environment around you and your perceptions become your reality. You essentially want to use your mind as a tool used to engage with life allowing us to experience emotions. You are not your mind, your mind is part of your soul. Over time using the mind as a tool will become easier. Most people do not even realize what is happening around them reflects what is going on in their mind. In my opinion, Ekhart Tolle said it the best, "Wherever you are, be there totally. If you find you're here and now intolerable and it makes you unhappy, you have three options: remove yourself from the situation, change it or accept it totally. If you want to take responsibility for your life, you must choose one of those three options and you must choose now. Then accept the consequences." When I originally read this statement it really made the light bulb go off for me. Every thought that I had, had an impact with the choice I was making, so I had to be willing to accept anything that came along with them. Think of your daily life as your school for your soul growth. The decisions you make daily in your life are leading you towards the reason you were brought to this wonderful planet. If you choose to not grow and surrender you will find that you will continuously relive the same cycles. The people may change, but the situations will be similar--remember that everything is energy and energy is always changing. The universe is going to continue to put things in your path that will require you to make decisions and how you choose to interpret them will be solely up to you. Free will to choose how you interpret situations is a tricky thing and everyone eventually has a breaking point. What I mean is that eventually everyone has a moment that brings them to the realization that they have no control over the things around them. The only thing a person can ever control is how they react to the things that are being sent their way.

One thing that is often overlooked is that happiness is an emotion, it is not a constant state of being. One of my favorite quotes was said by Denis Waitley, "Happiness cannot be traveled to, owned, earned, worn or consumed. Happiness is the spiritual experience of living every minute with love, grace and gratitude." Often, people postpone happiness by placing their happiness on external factors or conditions rather than following their internal feelings. Internal feelings come in the form of love and happiness within the heart and it is important to not allow external circumstances to be the foundation of your divine happiness. One must not chase happiness as external factors as it creates unattainable love and happiness. Have you ever said to yourself, "If I just get this job, I will be happy!" or "If I just make more money than I would be happy!" Conditions or external factors make happiness and love unattainable. One must create happiness because happiness cannot be found or chased. These are examples of us as humans chasing external happiness and gratification. However, the truth is, even when you receive those things, you are going to not feel as satisfied within yourself. This is why the true emotion of happiness needs to be created in the moments we are living right now. When was the last time you felt pure bliss and internal happiness? When we are experiencing happiness, we are making a choice to receive a moment as what is right for you. Seeing happiness in the moment causes a deep alignment within ourselves, our purpose and our chakras. This is why we sometimes have moments of pure appreciation for something, because we are listening to our divine being. It is seen as a deep sense of being aligned with your purpose. Our purpose for life is to feel this internal joy-- we are here to experience and manifest this through our soul contracts.

As I have mentioned prior, happiness comes from our heart chakras, but unfortunately, many of us are trained from a young age that happiness needs to be earned. I am here to tell you that "earning" happiness is the furthest thing from the truth. As we continue to move through this thing we call life and we have two choices, to choose happiness or to not. A great way to practice this is through gratitude, through daily affirmation and through sitting with your heart center. Gratitude is the most direct way to get in "contact" with the universe and bring you right back into the present moment.

Like any emotion, gratitude cannot be forced, but we can cultivate our thoughts so that gratitude is more likely to arise. Practicing gratitude helps create a HABIT where we focus on the positive in life. Gratitude leads to happiness and happiness leads to JOY! One way I practice bringing myself back into the moment is by doing what I like to call the 5 things of gratitude and you can do them anytime and anyplace. I simply look at my hand using my fingers and start by naming 5 things that I am grateful for. Some people may find it difficult to say things out loud, so practicing with a journal can be beneficial. Writing in your journal can also supply you with answers from the universe and allow you to go back and read all the things you have written.

35

No one said that walking a spiritual path was going to be easy but it is your choices and perspective that determine how you navigate it. Honestly, some decision you make will impact your life and those around you. However, opening yourself to this divine light allows you to see aspects of life that others cannot and this is because over time, you will vibrate on a higher frequency than others. With vibrating at a higher frequency than others, you will begin to experience not being able to differentiate between what are your emotions and what are others. Have you ever walked into a room of individuals and felt sudden energy or felt sick, but weren't sure why? Chances are you were picking up the energies of others around you. You need to recognize this in the moment and separate your energies from those around you. This is an excellent opportunity for you to empower yourself and make choices that serve your well being. A good choice in this situation is to ground your own energies is to focus on your environment and get back to the present. The method I prefer to use is actually getting outside in nature. If you do not practice this, it will cause you to feel overwhelmed and you will embody these energies as your own. Surrender the energies that are not yours to the universe and tell yourself that you release the energies of others and the energies that no longer serve you. Every day, you choose which vibrational plane you are going to vibrate on and you must set that intention for yourself every morning.

Whether you are at home, in your car on your way to work or walking, set the intention for your own energies. Remember, that whatever energy is within will be shown to you externally. So, if you do not set your vibration into a higher, more peaceful place, your surroundings and those around you will vibrate at that lower level. Empower yourself by providing yourself the opportunity to choose to approach life in the now. Allowing yourself the ability to be flexible and go with the flow as you are met with situations or obstacles. Never forget it is your right to have choices in regards to how you approach creating your life, why not make the choice to live it out of a place of peace, gratitude and love.

Learning to Love Yourself

Loving yourself seems like an easy task, right? NOPE, it can be exceedingly difficult! However, it is necessary in changing the world you see, especially if you grew up to believe that love has conditions. The truth is that loving yourself is a human necessity. Loving yourself is through how we take care of ourselves, how we support ourselves physically, mentally and spiritually. Without self-love, there is no growth and when there is no growth there is no end to reaching our divine purpose. Making a conscious effort to love yourself is one of the most important decisions you can make, when you love yourself first loving others comes easy. Allowing you to nurture and cultivate the world around you allows you to view the world with a new perspective. Allowing you to fall in love with life and yourself you learn to bring happiness and love back into your life it is then projected into the world around you. Unfortunately, many of us have been programmed to believe if you love yourself that you are vain, selfish, conceited and egotistical (just to name a few). The truth is when you start to find happiness in yourself and love yourself, loving others comes easy. It all starts with you!

Let us look in the mirror. Do you set conditions for yourself? Are they attainable? How would you feel if you finally were at your standard? Would you want more, or would you really feel fulfilled? I can only speak to my truth and vulnerability and I can tell you my answer to all these questions is, no. I have always felt in the past that I was looking for eternal validation, as if I was waiting for someone else or something else to dictate what was going to be the root cause of my happiness. If I never abandoned that idea, I would still be in a state of waiting. I ask you this: What conditions or external factors are you allowing to influence your current situation? What conditions have you set for yourself?

Some examples of conditions:

1. I cannot be loved by someone unless I look a certain way.
2. Love is based on how much money I have.
3. Love is based on the gifts I give.
4. Love is based on being physical or intimacy.
5. Love is based on how much I sacrifice for everyone else.
6. I cannot be loved by someone because I have too much baggage.
7. I cannot be loved by someone because I have things in my past that are unlovable.
8. I must not be loveable because I allowed _____ to happen.
9. There are so many more I can list.

Conditions are ideas that are programmed in us through our environment and upbringing through our childhood experiences. The outlook on how we perceive the world sits in a lot of our childhood traumas. These traumas have a direct correlation with how we see ourselves, how we interact with others, how we experience and execute change etc. I personally have had a hard time loving myself and discerning my emotions. Anytime I did something for myself I tend to associate it with guilt. I had been programmed to always give to others because the more you give to others the more, they will love you. Being programmed in such a way since I was younger was detrimental to not only myself, but my outward look on life. My truth sits in the fact that others will not love you for what you can give, love is a balancing game-- in order for there to be an abundance of love there needs to be a balance to giving and receiving.

The idea of changing my behavior seemed easy enough-- yeah, right! Changing my habits is the hardest thing I have ever decided to take on, especially when one of the habits I had to break was negative self-talk, body shaming and showing myself love. These things are deeply rooted in me in some of the deepest darkest parts of me. How was I supposed to love those parts of myself? This is still something I still get into entanglements within myself because healing from deeply rooted traumas and loving yourself is an ongoing process. It is not like you can just wake up one day and say I am going to love myself. I mean you can, but I assure you there is more to the process. There is a whole world around you, obligations, responsibilities and other factors that come into play.

Showing yourself love will look different for everyone. Looking inward at your own self-love and vulnerability is a difficult task, I know this. However, it is something that gets easier the more you practice. The more you practice, you will start to recognize love and compassion for your past and present self. Once you feel this, I assure you, you will notice loving yourself and others to be easy and in a place of calmness.

Self-Care

Self-care is one thing that must become a habit and routine. You will want to make sure that it is something that is maintainable. Something that you will enjoy doing. Self-care should not feel like a chore. I like to believe that over time the self-care routine becomes something you look forward to and brings you inner peace. This is important because on days when you are not feeling at your highest you will revert to old habits and routines.

1. Make sleep a priority.

2. Take care your gut

3. Exercise daily

4. Say no to others and say yes to your self-care.

5. Go outside with nature

6. Do something creative

7. Sing/dance

8. Meditate

9. Take a hot salt bath

10. Get a massage/pedicure/manicure even if it is done by yourself

11. Use affirmations

12. Be grateful for things you have and things you do not have

13. Write yourself a love note

14. Do something you find joy in

15. Clear out clutter

16. Schedule some alone time

17. Take a much-needed vacation (if that is an option)

18. Take a day off from social media and electronics

19. Introduce joy or humor into your day

20. Choose to do things because it is what you desire

The list just provides some ideas on how to create your own self-care routine. I suggest starting with one or two items, then incorporate more over time. It is extremely important that the self-care routine that you create works for you. At first, taking time for yourself and a self-care routine may seem awkward. If you are anything like me or resonate with me, you have put others' needs before your own for so long that you will have some growing pains with putting yourself first. You must remind yourself that it is for your highest good. Remember that your wants, needs and desires are valid and important.

Positive Affirmations

Another great practice that I used was implementing positive affirmations. Positive affirmations are statements that can be used to effectively challenge and overcome self-sabotaging thought patterns. Those behaviors we have justified over time, we all have them. I personally would rely on the need to find something wrong because it was too good to be true. Nothing came easy for me, so I would sabotage a situation by creating my own drama where none needed to be. It was because that is what I had known. Positive affirmations allow us to replace those thoughts.

Positive affirmations that I use:

1. I appreciate all the lessons that life has taught me.

2. I am confident and intelligent.

3. I naturally feel good about myself!

4. I am courageous and outgoing!

5. It feels good to feel good.

6. I choose to live my best life in alignment with my desires, standards and purpose.

7. My life is abundant.

8. I know myself and I honor my boundaries.

9. I choose to radiate self-confidence!

10. I accept and embrace myself for who I am.

You can use these statements throughout your day when you find that you are being challenged or triggered by old thought patterns or external factors. Overtime, you may find yourself slowly creating your own personal positive affirmations based on your own personal experiences. What people fail to know or understand about the human psyche is that the mind is programmable. So, essentially, after you tell yourself something over and over, the mind truly starts to believe it. Therefore, if you are speaking to yourself in a non-favorable way you are going to always see the non-favorable things.

When you begin your quest of daily affirmations, it will probably feel silly, strange and possibly meaningless, but I assure you these feelings will dissolve over time. When you first begin this affirmation process, you may not believe any of the positive affirmations that you are telling yourself, but being positive and persistent will make it easier over time. As the consistency continues, you will one day and the daily ritual of self-affirmation will become second nature-- this is a sign that your mindset has changed. The most euphoric and psychological feeling is the moment you catch yourself laughing and dancing with yourself in the mirror. Mind you, just because you come to this space of self-affirming awareness does not mean you will never think another negative thought again, you will just have the tool to dismantle the thoughts that do not serve your highest good. We all have these negative thoughts, even the most positive people have times where they experience doubt, insecurity, or thoughts that are not positive in nature.

A Love Letter

I have an assignment for you. Yes, you read that correctly, you have some homework to do. When I started pulling oracles cards for myself, I was led to this exercise and I found it to be an eye opening experience. The card I pulled spoke to how I was not what other people thought of me and how I need to remind myself that I have the power to influence the way that I not only talk to myself, but how other people speak to me. It showed me that I was deserving of human decency and loving words of affirmations from others. The realization hit me, if I could talk to myself in such a negative light, how could I expect others to speak to me with love and respect? If I could not talk to myself in such a manner how could I ever expect another person to talk to me that way. So, I started writing love letters to myself and I want to share this knowledge with you. So here is my assignment for you, I want you to write a love letter to yourself. In this love letter I want you to write everything and anything that you want to hear come out of another person's mouth towards you. When you bring your pen to paper, allow your thoughts to just flow, do not hold back the things you want to write. This is a chance for you to hear all the positive aspects of yourself that you needed to hear. Allow yourself to hear how amazing you are! I understand this is a difficult task, but it is necessary to utilize this tool to be able to refer to during your spiritual journey as a reminder to yourself that you are never alone.

I chose to lead by example, so I have included my love letter as an example.

Dear Chrissy,

Today I pulled a card and it told me I needed to write you a love letter. So, since the universe always delivers, I am listening. Here it goes. As I look into your beautiful green eyes, I see this beautiful softness. A vulnerability. It is mysterious and sexy. You draw me in. I see your strength on the outside, but it is your heart where your beauty can really be found. I know that you are hurting and do not allow those emotions to consume you. Feel them but do not become them. Give them up and do not dwell on them because I will love you. Forever and ever! I will be your rock. You will not need another. I choose you! You will be complete with me and together we will build the life you desire. Make sure to look in the mirror and admire what you see. When you feel lost and unwanted, look up at the sky and remember what matters. Was it the moments you felt unwanted that made you? No, those movements just brought you to this point. It was your heart that has always driven you. You are love. You must believe it. Remember that I love you. It has always been you. I will never let you down. I will never abandon you. I will always love you! Continue to be the amazing person you always have been. Lift others up and show them how to shine their lights too. You are so hard on yourself. It is time to open your eyes. See yourself through my eyes. See the radiant beauty that you are. Strong, loving, compassionate, worthy individual you are. Do not let another tear fall from those beautiful eyes of yours. Do not worry any more. Do not feel unworthy. I am here to tell you that I love you. I love all of you. You are everything I have ever wanted and all I ever dream about. It has always been you and will forever be you. Open your eyes, wake up, and smile because I am here. Together we will build what you have always dreamed.

I love you to infinity,

Chrissy

I know writing yourself a love letter is awkward, because I felt the awkwardness, too. It is okay to use this moment of writing to laugh with yourself, there is a sense of empowerment to laugh at yourself! Once you complete your letter, I want you to go back and read it. You will be so surprised at what it feels like to hear yourself talk to yourself in such a beautiful way. If you find that you cry, allow the tears to flow and allow yourself to feel the emotions that surface through the process. This exercise is a great step in relearning how to speak to yourself.

Knowing Your Energy

Everything in this world is energy, even yourself. One must be open to the idea that everything is energy and everything is an exchange of energy. Once you start to understand this concept, you will really begin to see the world in a whole new way. Tuning into your own energy, you will understand the external energies around you. Many ask, how do I feel my energy? The first thing I do and I suggest you do it too is, find a place where you are not easily disturbed. It is important to release any expectations you have of what may happen because expectations hinder the process. Make sure that you are in a comfortable position, sitting or lying comfortably whatever works best for you. Then you want to start with your breath slowly inhaling and exhaling. Taking a deep breath in holding it for 3 seconds and breathing it out through your feet. Pay attention and focus on any changes that are happening internally and externally such as sensations (sight, smell, taste, feelings, touch or hearing). One thing to preface is to not be discouraged if the first time you do not hear or feel anything, because again it is all about persistence and consistency. Every individual's experience is different, therefore, experiences tuning into one's energy differently. If this does not work for you, it is okay to try another technique.

Step 1: Find a quiet place where you will not be disturbed and just sit. Set the intention that this be done out of a place of love for yourself and for the energy around you. State out loud that you release any energy that is not yours that does not serve you on both the physical and non-physical level. Remind your body that nothing but love enters, and love remains. Remember, your intention in this message is important.

Step 2: Start to focus on your breath. Take a deep breath in hold it for 3 seconds and breathe it out through the feet. Continue to focus on the breath. Allow it to become a smooth & rhythmic in and out focusing on the rise and fall of your breathing point. As you focus on the breath you might begin to feel a change in the environment around you. Some might feel a tingling around the head/neck. Just pay attention to what you are feeling. (This can be done with your eyes open or closed).

Step 3: The next thing you are going to do is while still breathing place all your focus on your feet. Sending all your energy to your feet. Continuing to breathe. Deep breath in (hold for 2 seconds and deep breath out). Focus all your energy on your feet.

Step 4: Now, I want you to imagine that there is a glowing swirling white light of energy coming up from the earth into your feet. The energy is of the purest form straight from the earth. Feel the energy moving from the earth into your feet. Just feel the energy. Next, I want you to allow the energy to move up the legs, over the knees, through the thighs, over the hips, through the abdomen, into the chest, through the heart, over the shoulders, through the neck, up into the head and shooting up straight into the universe as far as you can imagine.

Step 5: You are now a direct line from the universe to mother earth. Feel the energy flowing through you freely. Now it is time to continue to make some mental notes. What are you feeling? What does your energy feel like? Did you feel any change in the environment around you? Do you see colors? Do you see images? Do you smell or hear anything? The experience is different for everyone. When you feel ready, focus back on the breath. Make sure to thank the universe for the experience. Start to wiggle your toes, fingers and other parts of the body. If you close your eyes, it is time to open them. If you decide to keep your eyes open, really look at the environment around you. Does it seem the same?

Step 6: Take a moment for yourself and just sit. Make sure you back in your surroundings and ready before you go and jump up and run off to the next thing. It is not uncommon to feel a little disoriented. Never do this when you really need to focus. (Like driving, operating machinery or anything that really requires 100% of your attention).

As I mentioned, this experience is different for everyone. You don't just need to sit for this practice, I do this sometimes when I am walking or while I focus on the flame of a candle. You need to focus on your breathing and allow yourself to experience the energy. Feel this energy deep within you, breathing from your root chakra-- imagine the breath going up through your whole body, building a relationship with your own energy. Building this relationship with your own energy is important for your own awareness and internal energy shift. As you do this more you will be able to see and feel energy more clearly and allow you to understand how it works for you.

Sitting and meditating can be a difficult process. There are many misconceived notions about meditation, one of those notions is the idea that an individual will not have any thoughts while in meditation. Our brains are wired for thoughts, therefore, this belief is simply not true. Over time it is about developing the ability to not acknowledge the thoughts and practicing saying, "I hear you" and stepping back into focusing on your breath. You are looking for answers where there is supposed to be mystery--but, knowing takes the joy out of your journey. There is so much more to this world that is still to be discovered, especially the world within yourself.

Boundaries

Boundaries, Boundaries, Boundaries! Once you start aligning yourself with your higher power, higher energies and start making decisions that are right for your life, it is important to start creating boundaries with yourself and others. Setting boundaries is a great way for you to decide what you are willing and not willing to tolerate or allow to impact areas of your life. Boundaries are for your well-being because in establishing boundaries you are growing and feeding your soul. Good defined boundaries allow you to cultivate an environment that is conducive to your growth.

Boundaries can be both physical and emotional. While physical boundaries can include aspects such as personal space and environment, emotional boundaries can be identified through actions that influence your self-worth that ultimately influences the decisions you make for your life. You can expect in the beginning when you start setting clear boundaries, those that the boundaries do not serve will definitely try to cross them. It will be up to you to stand firm, stand your ground and remember you have boundaries for a reason. Setting boundaries is not only setting you up to have a healthy relationship with yourself, but with other people. Unclear or lack of boundaries only set you up for allowing others to make decisions on what is or is not good for your life. You are entitled to your own thoughts and opinions. You are entitled to your own personal space. You are entitled to pursuing your goals and personal activities. You are entitled to your own spiritual beliefs.

You also must know your limits! There are going to be things that you absolutely will not accept. This requires you to look at how you currently do things. Pay close attention to how things impact your emotions, discussions and goals. Can you identify actions that you are taking or that may be hindering you from moving forward to completing your goals? Do you have any unfinished projects? Are you feeling extremely drained or tired after a particular interaction? You may decide that places that you once frequented you no longer feel comfortable at. The music you listen to may change and how you choose to interact with people may be different.

Setting boundaries is a great way for you to decide what you are willing and not willing to tolerate or allow to impact areas of your life. Of course, there are going to be times that we will have to deal with people, places or things that will not fully align with what we are trying to accomplish in our lives. When you find yourself in situations like this you may want to try a few techniques that have helped me.

Get in the practice of saying, NO! That is right, say NO! You do not have to do something that you do not want to do and remember it is not your job to please others. You cannot be afraid to say, "NO," especially if it does not align with your values or beliefs. Saying no does not mean you do not care about others and their feelings, it is about being honest with yourself and them when it comes to what is right for you.

Allow yourself to tune into your feelings. When you are first presented with something and you are feeling anxiety, resentment, physical pain or a gut feeling speak up. When creating these boundaries, make sure to be direct. You have a right to dictate what is or is not good for you. Make sure that you are clear with yourself and others when boundaries are being crossed, because failure to do so can result in confusion. You also do not want to hold on to the emotion and allow resentment to build because you did not speak up about boundaries being crossed.

Should you find that you are in a situation that you are being drained or responding emotionally, give yourself permission to take a time out. Sometimes we are not sure if something is for us right away--especially for those that have been people pleasing all their lives. Taking a time out and allowing yourself an opportunity to address what you may be feeling may be what you need before making decisions. Know that there is nothing wrong with taking time for yourself to gain clarity on a situation. After that time out you may find that you are ready to re-engage in a situation once you are aware of how you feel about it.

Like anything else, boundary work takes practice. If you are anything like me, you may resonate by putting other people before yourself. When you start to create boundaries, you may experience guilt or even feel a little selfish. You may even worry that some may see you as rude or self-centered because this is not your normal behavior. If you find that you are being met with this new behavior is about respecting yourself, honoring your needs, wants and desires. It is about being honest with yourself and honest with others while maintaining your inner peace.

Whole Being Work

There are magical things happening around you. I ask you what has kept you from seeing all the good that is right in front of you? What is hindering your ability to listen and trust your intuition? It is not the job of another to tell you who or what you are supposed to be doing. Part of your path is for you to discover yourself and really believe that the universe supports you. There is only one true way for self-discovery and that is to start asking yourself the hard questions. Stop procrastinating hoping that you will stumble upon an answer. Stop wasting your time trying to find validation in the words and concepts of others. Ask yourself why you do the things you do. Is it because someone else told you that is how it should be? You must do more, be more, or give more? Is what you are doing really making you happy and feeling fulfilled? What do you really value and what excites you? All the answers you seek are already inside you, just dig deep to uncover them. Take a deep breath and be patient with yourself, this is not something that can be rushed.

We all have parts of ourselves that need healing. Your shadow side will always be a part of you. It is not like you can detach it and throw it away, so you must accept it. Love the shadow part of you like you would the light part. Remember the light needs the dark just like the dark needs the light--there is beauty in both. Accept the parts of you that you look upon or have been programmed to believe are unfavorable and trust the universe's guidance. Do not get lost in the thoughts, you must feel your way through this process. Feel and identify the emotions and accept them. I cannot stress enough, experiencing emotions is part of the human experience. Trust when I tell you, even within myself there are parts of me I do not want others to see. Yes, I can be a mean person and there are people who would tell you that I am a mean person that is their own perception. At the time, I was probably mean to them and did something to them that did not align with their beliefs and values. Overall, I try my absolute best to treat people well. I never set an intention that I am going to hurt-- it is not like I set my intention that I am going to hurt others. However, that does not mean it will not happen. Even in these moments I realize I am human like everyone else. Sometimes I can be hot headed and let my mouth run away with me that is for sure. One thing that my awakening has taught me is that I must accept myself for it. During these times, I must ask myself the following questions: Why did I get hot headed? What was being triggered now? What part did I play in the situation? I mean the real part. Not my side of the story part. When was the first time I felt that emotion? I identify it and I let it go. I release the guilt, judgement and self-imposed attachment to it and release it up. I release this guilt to the universe and ask for healing and clarity in these moments. That does not mean that I am never triggered again, it means that I have identified the why and now I can accept the part I played.

Many people ask me, "How did you start accepting the qualities of yourself that you hide from the world?" I accepted these qualities by doing the things I mention throughout the book. I faced them through journaling and associating the actions with emotions that I was feeling. I also had to come to terms and accept I was not going to be the good in everyone's story. There are times that I was manipulative, self-centered and aloof (just to name a few). It required me to accept that I have those qualities and love myself for them. Truth be told, everyone can get suffocated in these actions as well.

There are points in our lives where we are asked to go inward and reflect. During these times of reflection, you may begin to look at yourself and how your actions impacted a situation. This action allows us to be present in the moment and in this time, it is particularly important to not allow yourself to know what is going wrong. In these moments, remind yourself not to dwell on the dream of the present because this will only bring you further into distress. The important part to practice here is to clear your mind and not get lost and internalize the key is to clear the mind. Allow your guilt to propel you forward and motivate positive change in your behaviors. Internalizing it will only inhibit you from forward movement. When you hold on to guilt it keeps you reliving the past and you project it out only to relive it over and over.

You must acknowledge the role you play in situations you find yourself in. Why did you play that role? Were you the victim? Were you the manipulator, instigator or reactor? Were you trying to gain something from the situation? What were you trying to accomplish during that time and how could you have approached the situation differently if it presented itself again in the future?

How you respond to a situation is a choice and an opportunity to empower yourself in the now. If you respond from a place of fear or emotional distress, we then allow our emotions to control us and control how we move forward. This inhibits us from using our abilities and allows us to settle for less than what we deserve. Sometimes this can manifest into our lives as sleepless nights, not wanting to get out of bed, being preoccupied, overthinking, obsessive thoughts and feeling discouraged.

If this is the case in your life, remember that you are NOT your emotions. You are a soul that experiences emotions, but does not have to live them. Acknowledging your feelings does not mean you have to act on them. Use it as an opportunity to learn a lesson so you are not asked to repeat the pattern again. Instead of acting out on your emotions try this instead. Speak the truth about what is going on in your life. This can be extremely uncomfortable at times, but it is about being honest with yourself. Have compassion for yourself and others. We are human and are not perfect, nor are we expected to be. This allows you to release the judgement you impose on yourself and in some cases on others. Be curious about the experience in the now and identify your fears. You might experience some tension between what you know and what can be. This experience of tension within yourself is expected at times, but in these moments try to replace discomfort with excitement. Replace this discomfort with excitement. Yes, you read that correctly, replace it with excitement. Get excited with the idea that discomfort is temporary and you have the power to choose to approach life or situations differently today compared to yesterday. Use the discomfort as an opportunity to observe the present moment and what you are now choosing. There is freedom in that process.

A person manifests things both good and bad into their life repeatedly until they abandon an old way of thinking and adopt a new perspective. In the book, *Dancing with the Universe* by Dianne Rosena Jones specifically discusses her fear of abandonment. While reading it I had my own epiphany!

"Your fear of abandonment will manifest and lurk in every corner of every intimate relationship until you abandon it!"

Dianne Rosena Jones

When I read this quote, I took what she said and interpreted it even further. The thought immediately came to my mind that if you can manifest your fear into a relationship, you can manifest your fear into every part of your life. This means that what you fear will continue to show up in your life.

For this to change a person must do a couple things:

>Identify the fear and the source.

>Address it.

>Release it.

>Reprogram the belief.

Easier said than done, I know. Identifying, addressing, releasing and reprogramming requires an individual to really do some soul searching. The only way to overcome these tasks is to turn the attention inward. Turning inward can feel scary and a ridiculously hard task but it requires one to be honest with themselves. Sometimes being honest with yourself is the hardest thing to do because it requires one to be vulnerable and open yourself to relive traumas and ideas that may have been carried for most of a lifetime or in some cases longer. To be honest one of the hardest concepts I have come to grips with is, people form their identities based on the traumas they have lived. An example of something I used to say to myself was "I am worthless because I do not live up to the belief and standards that I have set for myself or have allowed to be influenced by others." The fact is that belief is far from the truth. It only becomes valid if I place value on it. You must ask yourself hard questions, such as: Why do you give it value? What is it really triggering? Is this something that I believe or is it a belief I can let go of? If you find you cannot let go of it then you must go deeper and you must ask yourself what is prohibiting you from releasing it. It will continue to manifest in your life until you fully release it. That is the answer to the question why I am finding myself in the same situation repeatedly.

What are you holding on to? Look at the patterns that are happening in your life and you will find that they are a product of something you are holding on to -- this can be both good and bad. If the pattern is something that creates positivity and allows you to continue to grow, then it is something to keep and cultivate. If it is something that is keeping you from growth and forward movement it is time to turn inward for answers. Identify, accept, release and reprogram!

The overall goal of shadow work is to fully accept yourself unconditionally. Everyone has things they do not consider favorable qualities. Once you can fully accept that in yourself, accepting it from others becomes a far easier task. Do your best to focus on self-compassion and acceptance of your own humanness. Laugh at yourself daily and try not to take everything so seriously. Sometimes instilling laughter is the easiest way to navigate through the process.

Keep the idea in your mind of your good qualities and accept the possibility that the opposite may also be true. To truly accept you must be willing to be aware that you are capable of the opposite of what you consider good. Only focusing on the good/ positive side is easy and comfortable. It is much easier to overlook and internalize our shadow side. What most fail to realize is that the shadow side will manifest in your relationships until they are identified and accepted.

When I was doing my shadow work, I went to the lengths of giving my shadow side a nickname. My shadow side is, Teenie. She likes to create chaos by making experiences far more difficult than they actually are. When she is faced with tasks that require patience, not getting her way and when she feels the need to play the victim. Being able to identify when my shadow side is being made present allowed me to identify when I was being triggered allowing me to identify the need to become more aware of how I was responding in those moments.

Journaling also is a great creative way to do your shadow work. To be honest, how I do my shadow work is something I get asked regularly. I absolutely love journaling because journaling allows me to release emotion. It allows you to reflect on events and as you begin to write sometimes it uncovers things that you did not even know were beneath the surface.

I personally found that the journaling was a great way to begin. First go into a store to buy a journal. When picking your journal make sure it is one that fits your personality-- something you are going to want to keep and look back on. Your journal and you should have a bond, after all, you are going to write some very intimate things in it. Turn to the first page and start by setting your intention. I personally set my intention for it to bring inspiration and healing to myself/life. Then when you are ready start with a topic.

I have listed some topics I used, but there is no rhyme or reason to how you do your journal. If structure is what you need then start with day one. If you need ideas feel free to use them however fits your needs. There is no wrong way to do it. It is your journey so I must be something that works for you.

Journal Topics

1. If present day me could talk to myself from 5 years ago, I would say…

2. How I spend my days is how I will spend my life. How do I feel about that?

3. My ideal day starts with…

4. Getting triggered unexpectedly can be a positive thing because…

5. When I think about my life in the present, I am most proud of…

6. Money and success are byproducts - not the goals - of my unique expression.

7. What are the current and recurring problems in my life? What would happen if I started viewing problems as opportunities?

8. What I want and what I need are not always the same. Provide examples.

9. A rejection can point me in the right direction. An example of this in my life is…

10. When I think about my future, I am most excited about…

11. If I'm feeling stressed because?

12. I constantly feel like I must be perfect because?

13. I cannot fix, change or improve anyone. How can I lead by example?

14. True wellness involves _____.

15. The opposite of depression is not happiness, is it?

16. Do I actively listen from my heart? Or do I analyze with my mind? Why?

17. Mindfulness turns habits into rituals and ceremonies.

18. I feel happy and confident when I …

19. I want recognition for…

20. I wish others understood this about me…

21. What does 'freedom' mean to me?

22. I felt valued and loved when…

23. When I think about my future, I feel?

24. Do I project aspects of myself onto others?

25. I feel happiest in my skin when…

26. Who is my 'highest self'?

27. The way I define my values has changed…

28. I feel energized when…

Your Words Have Power

In addition to changing the narrative that you allow to replay in your mind, I would also like to bring your attention to the words that you speak. Words have so much power, that is why it is essential to always speak what you want, not what you do not want.

Let me paint you a picture. I found that in my relationships there was a constant back and forth of pointing blame. I would repeatedly speak about things that I did not want to experience in the relationships. For instance, with friends I would say things like, "I do not always want to be the one that has to reach out first." Another thing I would say is, "I do not want to be talked down to or undermined in front of the children." I soon noticed the more that I spoke or thought about what I did not want, the more of what I did not want happened. Remember, the Universe is going to deliver exactly what you put your feelings and beliefs into. If you are putting your feelings and belief into something that you do not want, you are telling the Universe to deliver it.

Start speaking what you do want! I will demonstrate using the situation I just described. Instead of saying, "I do not want to always be the one that reached out first," I would now say, "I would like to have balanced relationships where the other person wants to talk to me as much as I want to talk to them." You must be clear in your delivery, the Universe will not sort through it for

71

you. It will deliver whatever you place the most feeling into. Keep that in your mind when you are trying to move from where you are now to what you want.

I talked to you about a love letter. Remember that your spiritual journey starts in the mind, but leads you to fulfill the desires of the heart. This chapter I will discuss with you the importance of creating your manifesto. Basically, if you do not know what a manifesto consists of your values, ideas, goals, desires, resources, internal/external influences, spiritual guidance needed. This manifest is basically a written declaration of who you are. What do you want to achieve? What can you do to complete your goal and what do you require to complete it? Think of it as your vision of yourself and what you want for your life. It stems from the idea that manifest basically means to, make appear. The idea behind the manifesto is you will put the vision you have for your life into words. This visualization technique assists by officially asking the universe to allow your dreams and hearts desires to materialize.

I am sure you are thinking, you cannot just put words on a piece of paper and then expect things to just start happening. You would be correct, it is more than that. You will manifest the thoughts that you focus on the most in your life. This method allows you to focus and visualize your thoughts in a more positive light. The more serious you are about your vision (feeling you put behind it), the better the likelihood of them coming to fruition.

Most people focus on abundance (world items), appearance, healthier, career and relationships.

Regardless of what you envision for your life, there is no wrong in whatever you are asking for-- it is your life and your heart's desire. It is ultimately what is going to bring you into the state of joy this lifetime. So, I encourage you as you do this to not feel shame, guilt, or fear when you are setting goals. The only thing you need to ask yourself is, do you feel joy at the thought of you having the things you desired? If you can answer yes, that is all that matters, and you know that your vision is clear.

The outline that I personally use with my manifesto will be included at the end of this chapter. A manifesto is a great way to place your wants out into the Universe to create that life that makes you go, WOW!

You will be amazed at how quickly things start to happen and manifest once you make a declaration out of your mind into the world. When I wrote my first manifesto-- yes, I said my first because after I wrote my manifesto-- I found that I referred to it often to help remind myself where I was going and how I planned to do my part. It was then as I started to grow, I found that who I was at the core was different than I originally thought. Which led me to revise my manifesto over time. It made sense to me considering we are all energy and constantly experiencing change/transformation. Not to mention that as I would start to take the steps that I could in the now, I would find that some things would work and others would not. I never considered the things that did not work and I did my best. I just did my best to roll with the punches. Trying to see disappointments or roadblocks as a pause in a project. In some instances, I would be led to a solution that would work better. Do not get discouraged if you find that what you first write you go back and change, it is perfectly fine. Changing your manifesto just means that you are stepping into a new idea of who you are on the soul level.

Writing your manifesto can at times be a difficult process and it also should not be taken lightly as words hold a lot of power. It is important to be clear that what you are envisioning is something that you will be pleased with receiving, even if things or ideals change over time. If you find that you are having a hard time or going blank, it is okay to walk away and revisit with a new idea or clear mind. Do not be afraid to ask for guidance, because when you go within and ask for guidance it will be given.

Be open to the ideas that come to your mind after asking for guidance, taking some time to reflect on them. I found that when guidance came it was best for me to write it down allowing time for reflection before I acted upon it. If at any time you are met with fear, spend some time with your vision clarifying why or where you are feeling the most fear. While I was taking a spiritual coaching course, they explained fear as the false, ego, appearing, real (FEAR). I thought this was an excellent acronym that explained what it meant to be living in fear. Basically, what I received and applied when I was writing my manifesto was that I let old belief systems keep in place from moving forward. I was allowing my ego to keep me from dreaming big and playing it safe? Were the values, beliefs, ideas and thoughts of others keeping me in a place of not believing I was worthy of having a dream? Therefore, feeding me reality that was false and not in alignment with made my soul happy. One of the most important things is to remember that you are not your past, do not and I repeat do not let your past dictate your dreams and what shapes your life in the now. You must really know why you want something. What is the reason behind it?

The technique I am going to mention consists of looking to the past, but this is only to propel you forward. Even some past disappointments can be good motivators in assisting in propelling you forward because they allow you to look at how you may want to do something different. A good technique to assist with overcoming the fear you may experience is looking back on time where you have had successes with previous situations and goals. Allow these successes to bring you back to where you are now and assist in motivating you as you continue with the process.

Reality is, every dream that a person ever had was just that, a dream. A figment of the imagination that was placed out into the universe with the belief that it could be accomplished. Yes, there is always work to be done but never sell yourself short. When you are composing your manifesto, you do not need to waste time worrying about how it will happen. Just the emotion and feeling of achieving it.

Envision your manifesto as a blueprint. It provides you the opportunity to openly discuss with the universe what you want for your life out in the open. It helps you with visualizing where you want to go. Do not rush it, take your time, but come back and revisit and revise if you feel drawn to. As you continue to learn more about yourself you will find that things you once thought were in alignment with you may no longer fit.

Writing your Manifesto

Who are you now? (The good, the bad, the ugly? Really investigate what you like about yourself and pay special attention to what you do not like.) The overall goal is to love all of yourself unconditionally. Where do you want to be? What is your life plan? (This could be short term, long term, or spiritually) Remember it is all about you and the world you see. What do you forgive yourself for? Make sure that not only do you forgive yourself you set the intention to release it but, let it go. What do you forgive others for? Set the intention to not only forgive them, but release and let go of it. What is holding you back? These are obstacles you are knowingly aware of. Allow yourself to live in the moment, you must also accept that you are not limited by your current circumstances so when you are envisioning, envision big.

Before sitting down and writing your manifesto I suggest doing a mediation. Ask your higher self to assist you in writing it. This can be done during meditation, prayer or any form of communication that feels comfortable for you. I suggest this because you want your manifesto to be shaped based on your passions and the things that bring you joy. Our lives and plan for our lives should consist of the things that will bring the utmost joy to the soul. The first part of your manifesto should be who are you? It is a hard question to ask oneself, I know. This takes a lot of reflection, but this is when you get down to the core of who you are, what you value, what you believe. These are the qualities and attributes, belief systems, values, morals that you find important. If you were going to describe yourself because you were being interviewed without an expectation of what you had to be, how would you describe yourself? When you are asking yourself who you are you may want to make a list. Things that you value and why you value them. What are your values? The values and beliefs that you put into your manifesto really impact how things are delivered because your authentic self is rooted in what you value. Remember, your values are the core of who you are! Therefore, it is extremely important to identify what you place your belief in. It is your belief that gives your manifesto its power. The more belief you put behind it the more the universe works its magic to deliver. There is a good chance that you will have to dig deep to identify what it is you really value. This is because many have been deeply influenced by our family and society. When it comes to our Values, there is no right or wrong - only who WE are!

Were any of your values influenced by internal or external values? A great example of this would be to always have to give more in order to receive. Do you believe this because you were taught that by family or conditions experienced from important relationships in our lives? An external factor would be something that you have no control or influence over. This could be the physical environment or even social belief systems. Do you consider these favorable or unfavorable? If so, Why? It is good to look at these because when you go to write your manifesto you are the author. You can write your declaration as you see fit as this is designed to assist you in growing your soul. Remember, it is your intention in this message that is important because it is your soul and your life. You get a say in the dreams that are chased and how your life gets lived. Why not make it the best possible life it can be? Never forget, the universe says, "yes" the mind says, "no". The only limitations that you have are the limitations you place upon yourself. I hope that this tool assist you in discovering the limitless being you were always meant to be.

Example Template for Manifesto

WHO ARE YOU (qualities and attributes):

_____
_____
_____
_____
_____

WHAT DO YOU VALUE (beliefs, morals, and passions):

_____
_____
_____
_____
_____

INERNAL INFLUENECS:

Favorable:

_____
_____
_____
_____

Non Favorable:

_____
_____
_____
_____

EXTERNAL INFLUENCES:

Favorable:

_____

_____

_____

_____

_____

Non Favorable:

_____

_____

_____

_____

_____

DEFINE YOUR GOAL:

_____

_____

_____

_____

_____

_____

_____

_____

_____

_____

_____

_____

THE CURRENT SITUATION:

_____
_____
_____
_____
_____

WHAT GUIDANCE IS NEEDED TO MOVE FORWARD?

_____
_____
_____
_____
_____

WHAT RESOURCES DO YOU NEED?

_____
_____
_____
_____
_____

WHAT RESOURCES ARE AVAILABLE NOW?

_____
_____
_____
_____
_____

IDENTIFY ACTIONS YOU CAN TAKE IN THE PRESENT MOMENT TO WORK TOWARD YOUR GOAL:

_____

_____

_____

_____

_____

_____

_____

_____

_____

_____

Surrender and Trust in Divine Timing

Sometimes we can get so focused on where we want to go, that we lose where we are now. Where we are now is the most important place to be. This is where we are building foundations, planting our seeds and learning the lessons we came here to learn. Building these foundations and learning these lessons happen, so when we get to the destination, we can be in a place to receive it fully. Do your best to stay in a state of trusting that the universe will provide the opportunities that are meant for you. This means people may show up and resources may become available. You must surrender and allow them to unfold as they will and know you cannot force or rush things to happen. Stay flexible in allowing for things to end up bigger and better than you could have ever envisioned and allowing yourself to surrender to being flexible allows for opportunity. If you fail to fully surrender and remain flexible you may overlook things that were meant to be seen.

Trying to control the path is in a sense cheating yourself. It is not a time to sell yourself short, it is a time of great change for you, and it is not meant for you to know all the time. You have to release the fear of the unknown and find excitement in the mystery. Everyone goes through times where they are unclear and confused of the why associated with the changes that are happening around them. During this time, please do not give up--

stay true to your faith and trust the process. Like any process, you must go through every step for it to be a successful process and do not try to rush the finished product. If you must reflect and see progress, go back and read your journal. Take the time to return to your breath and find guidance through your mediation.

When you try to control outcomes or situations you are telling the Universe that your way is the best way. This is telling yourself and the universe that where you are right now is exactly where you want to stay. The Universe does not consider stagnancy an option. You only have two options, either you grow or you regress. Which one is it going to be? If you find that you are feeling a state of anxiety you are holding on to the outcome too much and living for the future. If you find that you are experiencing fear or resentment you are too much in the past. When this happens, you need to come back center by returning to your breath. Breath is the key to life, it helps bring calmness, clarity and helps bring you back to your center. So, it is pertinent that you surrender to this process. When you need a sign that you are on the right path ask for a specific sign. The universe and your spiritual team are there for you always so if you are feeling disconnected ask for guidance. The guidance will always come. When you ask for your sign, be specific by choosing an object that has meaning to you. The way I do it is I will say, "Thank you for always being there for me. I currently feel disconnected or unsure right now, will you please let me know that I am making decisions for my highest good by sending me a rose." I personally like to select objects that are difficult to find to ensure that the sign is for me. You might think a rose would not be hard to find but when I selected a rose it was winter so seeing a rose in nature would be difficult. Just trust that the signs will come, in my scenario after I had let the thought go I came downstairs to a picture of a rose that my daughter had drawn and left it on the table for me so, trust that the guidance you need will come.

When you are feeling overwhelmed or it is too hard, remember you do not have to do it alone. In the moment of franticness or feeling overwhelmed, do not try to control it, but surrender. Surrender your desire out to the universe, come back to self through meditation and listen for guidance. Once you surrender you will begin to see the signs that you are in alignment. Keep in mind that signs are always secondary to the request. Some signs are often expressed through the words of people you are interacting with. It can be through repetitive numbers often referred to as angel numbers. It could be through the lyrics of music or even pictures.

In order to surrender, you must surrender totally and believing in yourself is the objective. Remember, you are creative and have the power inside you to overcome this obstacle, just trust that the universe will always show up. Do not worry about how everything is going to happen in the future. All yourself to internalize and really embody the belief that you deserve all that you want and desire. You must come back to self, release control and surrender to the will of the universe.

Things are not meant to always be black and white. You are looking for answers where there is supposed to be mystery-- knowing takes the joy out of your journey. There is so much more to this world that is still to be discovered. Explore this world with childlike excitement and allow yourself to see it with new eyes. Seeing life in a new scope will bring knowledge and new inspiration to the surface. To get the true answers that you need, there is only one way to do so. As, you must look inward because ALL the answers you seek are inside of you and will be shown in divine timing. You are not meant to find out who you are in a report, you are meant to discover that on your own. Understand the possible why something may potentially happen allowing for the present to fill with passion and feeling, do not get too attached to the how. Worrying about the how can lead you away from what is meant for you. It is important to note that our path is never set in stone. So, utilize the tools to overcome challenges you will face that will help you as you turn inward to find answers. It is okay to be curious and want to know about everything because, in the end you will be able to identify what is for you and what is not.

Let's go back to a few significant events in your life, I want you to look at this from a larger scale. Choose a few significant events in your life. When I say significant, I mean the ones that have shape or really had an impact on where you are now. I want you to think how choices and timing played a vital role on how they played out. If any timing would have been different would you have received some of the blessings or memories that you hold dear to you? I will use a few events in my life that divine timing played an important role. I wanted to share my knowledge with others in regards to my awakening to assist in their awakening. I had no idea how or when this would happen. What I did know was I needed to grow my knowledge because I wanted to help others heal and live an abundant life. I did not know where to start or what to look for. What I began to do in the beginning of my journey was, I started to look for signs around me in my day to day life. I had already had the immense feeling that I was supposed to share my knowledge with others and because I felt that deeply, I was beginning to manifest opportunities for growth into my life.

I met a spiritual teacher that I met through social media and I took a leap of faith and decided to take one of her intuition classes. I waited for the classes and zoom sessions so I could express what I was experiencing hoping to gain insight. From there she explained that I, like many others, were going to experience awakenings because it was what our souls came to earth to do. If I was to be totally honest, when she first said this, I had truly little belief and a lot of doubt. So, at this moment I decided to listen and take some notes. I could not help but to think about all the dreams that were coming true and how I was experiencing a lot of synchronicities prior to this class. My spiritual teacher gave my class some pointers and a little direction. However, the real growth started coming along when I really allowed my intuition to lead the way. Soon after my class I was led to a book and on my search for knowledge. The more that I would complete a step that was leading me to help and teach others the more opportunities were being presented at just the right time. So, I began writing this book. The intention behind the thought of this book was to teach others how to sit and understand their awakening and let them know they were not alone. As I started writing something did not feel right, so I stopped and was shown another route. My interpretation was that there must be something missing, so I took the new road presented to me.

I started to do personal readings on social media for free. The first time I did this I had one hundred free readings to give. As I began to give the readings people would leave reviews--I saw these as confirmation. This was confirmation that teaching and leading others was the path I was supposed to take. I told myself even if my path only healed myself, I would consider it a success.

Due to the response of the readings, I decided the idea of getting a business license came to mind. I had no idea how or why I needed one, but it was like the steps were being laid as I walked them. October 22, I got my business license. Although I really didn't have a plan on how I was going to accomplish it or what I was even building, I was led to get my business license. Right after I got my business license I did a reading for a young lady and her boyfriend. After the reading she mentioned how her boyfriend did not have a social media platform and wanted to leave a review on my webpage. I had just had the vision of creating a webpage but had no idea how or where to start. It turned out she was well versed in the task and provided me guidance on where to start. Two days later I created my first webpage with no prior training. The story continues but the morale is that everyone that encounters us is either an opportunity to learn or teach. The universe will nudge us in the direction we need to go but it is up to us to be open to the opportunities when they are presented. Those nudges are divinely timed through the interactions we have with the people, places and things we interact with.

You Only Get One Life

Getting caught up in life is very easy to do. What does it mean to not take life so seriously? Well, it means that we should not dwell on what is happening to us. It is about allowing ourselves to keep moving. Knowing that although things that seem unfavorable for what we want in life may happen to us so will favorable things. So, be willing to go with the flow and let some things go.

We forget that there is a time where we have to be serious but, enjoying life is just as important. Sometimes things are just not going to work out, which means that there are going to be days that life is going to slap us in the face. There are times when you might just want to look up at the sky and ask the universe "WHY ME?" Use those moments to laugh-- at yourself for looking up at the sky for asking why. Then laugh at the universe for having a sick sense of humor. Yes, sometimes the universe will throw something at us just to show us we can do it.

One thing I have learned is that we only get one life. Each one of us is a unique puzzle piece to this world we live in. All of us have something special that we contribute to this world. I ask what that special thing inside you is. What are you putting out into the world or are you allowing the world to control your life? There is no other you in this whole entire universe. You have a perspective unlike another. You have a whole life to live, so why not make it the best life ever.

Explore this world with childlike excitement and allow yourself to see it with new eyes. Get in touch with your inner child and allow your creativity to flow out of you. This will bring knowledge and new inspiration to the surface. It is OKAY to be curious and want to know about everything, we've all been trained. We've all been trained to believe that knowledge is power. Knowledge will give you the ability to see things from different viewpoints. Seeing aspects of life allows you to see things from different perspectives. As you learn and grow with yourself and the world you see, you will notice not everything resonates with you and that is okay. As you begin to really identify what it is you believe in and place value on you will be led to people or situations needed.

Keep in mind sometimes we are also led to the opposite of what we wanted, but this is merely an opportunity as confirmation from the universe that those "things" are not meant for us. In the end you will be able to identify what is for you and what is not. When you are unsure, ask for a sign and it will be delivered. The method I used to ask for a sign is I will pick two different objects, one to identify yes and the other to represent a no. Trust and have faith that the universe will support you as you continue to allow your authentic self to be seen. As you continue to trust and align the universe will continue to show up -- just open your heart and allow the universe to lead you. As you learn your lessons and find new ideas, share them with others. The most important thing to remember is your belief in something gives the object power.

If you are looking for answers in a book or through knowledge, it is your belief in that book or series of words in the book that give it meaning. For example, have you ever heard of someone trying to change a partner or someone in their life? People will not change just because an individual wants them to because this is not a belief the other has about themselves. Once a person holds and places power in something then and only then does something have power. The true power comes in the feeling and belief of a thing, concept or an idea.

Lift others up and assist in leading them by sharing the knowledge you receive during your journey. Allow yourself to love without conditions and cultivate your abundant life. I find joy and fulfillment in watching others live the life they desire.

Believe in yourself! Love yourself unconditionally is the key to connecting to a source and remember, everything is energetically connected. We are all part of this great universe and the universe is part of us. So, treating yourself with respect, kindness, compassion and acceptance living out of a place of non-judgement is the key to maintaining a frequency that aligns with the frequency of the universe. Keep in mind, our internal world is reflected in our external world-- what we put out always finds its way back to us. Always receive your energy from source by aligning with the higher frequencies. Being in a higher soul vibration allows you to use your energy in such ways that benefit all that you encounter. All souls have a divine purpose and their life is their purpose. Love is the key to the return of humanity that the return starts with everyone being. Forgiveness is never for the receiver but for the person forgiving. Forgiving yourself for past judgements, actions, and sabotaging behaviors is the key to releasing blockages. In forgiving yourself, it allows you to create your heaven within. This allows each person to receive and live their abundant life in the now. Self-reflection allows for the identification and clearing of all blockages. This is on both the physical and non-physical level. It is key to remember that we are not the decisions of others, we are only the decisions that we make. Our actions are the only actions that we can control in our lifetime. Every action, every decision is your energy used to shape your life. It is important to use your energy in the most positive ways to ensure the universe can deliver the life you are destined to live.

Healing yourself will naturally help heal those around you. The world as you know it will start to change drastically. Showing yourself compassion allows for you to show compassion for others. Loving yourself allows you to love others. Release all fears, judgements and guilt associated with the past because the past is no longer. The future has not yet arrived, there is only right now this present moment so how present do you want to be?

Speak your truth and be mindful with your thoughts and words. Your thoughts quickly become your reality. Your words will not only influence your life, but the life of others. Honoring your truth must be done in such a way that you honor yourself and your emotions. Realize that your truth and desires may not always align with others. Not aligning with people any longer is to be expected because everyone is on their own path. However, it is important to remember that they also have a truth and that it is not your place to judge. It is your place to accept they are just on a different path and have not yet learned or understand yet. Show others they are still worthy of love and see them for who they are because people deserve to be loved for just existing.

Do not be afraid of releasing things that no longer serve you, because sometimes things just are not meant for you any longer. Trust that what is yours will always return to you, just believe and have faith. Those that love you, will find you. It is your job to be grateful for what you have now so when you receive your destiny you will understand the true value of how you got there. The present moments are the key to unveiling that destiny. So be present. Tell those you love you love them. Make it known that you are there even if they cannot hear you.

Opportunities will arise, take the opportunity and know that every person you encounter will have a purpose. There is a lesson to learn or a message to receive from everyone and you must be open to the lesson and allow them to guide you forward on your journey. Life will not always be easy and that is because there are lessons to be learned. During these times do not act in haste, let the chaos subside and come at it with a clear mind. Sit with yourself and listen to your inner voice. It will never lead you astray. The hard lessons in life are the ones where you gain the most wisdom. Your darkest moments will be the moments that inspire others. One really important thing in this journey is resting, because resting allows self-care and energy to push you forward through your healing and challenging moments. Make sure to take care of yourself and make it a priority because you are worthy of rest and worthy to be cared for. When you make yourself a priority you are telling others that you are deserving. Realize you cannot always be the giver and that you deserve to receive, too. In the past you have always given everything to others and have always accepted less in return. Those days are no longer! Continuing to give with no expectations will allow you to receive, so be a good receiver. You are just as deserving as everyone else, so do not compare yourself to others--you can never be another and another can never be you. There is only one you in the universe and you are that missing piece to the puzzle. There is no one that can ever be or love like you because your love is special, your love heals. Your love is the most special kind of love because it is unconditional. It is the love that releases all judgments and meets people on the most intimate level and you must allow others to show you this love too. When you begin to receive, do not close yourself off, continue to cultivate the light inside you. As you begin to let your light shine others may become uncomfortable. If this happens do not dim your light to make them happy, that will just give your power away. Continue to break the habits of negative self-talk and replace it with favorable self-assurance. Do not lose sight of your passion because your passion leads you to your destiny.

Working hard is normal. Do not forget to enjoy the achievements that have been afforded to you. Acknowledge and appreciate the achievements that you accomplish because these are the foundations of where you are going. The life you always dreamed is happening for you. See it! Envision it! Know it! Believe in it!

Decide today that you are going to choose yourself and chase your dreams. Your past does not have to define you. Yes, this may mean that people will leave your life but that does not mean they are gone forever, it may just mean right now. Continue to trust that what is meant for you is always yours--even if it is just for a moment, it was still yours. No one can ever take these moments away from you, the only limiting thing in your life is the thoughts and beliefs that you hold inside.

Consider your mind the prison and your thoughts are the warden. The Universe wants you to know that changing the way you view the world around you is not an easy process. However, it is without a doubt fulfilling in the end. Remember it is the mind that tells us no. The Universe always says, "YES!"

You do not need to know how you are going to get there, what the journey will look like or how things will come, you need to believe that it is already yours. Take the leap of faith and do the things that you can in the moment. Sometimes those things will require you to act and make some hard decisions, while other times you will do nothing but rest. Surprisingly, resting is doing something. Others will not understand and remember it is not your job to make them understand. This journey is for you to jump head first and go for your dreams allowing your heart to lead. It is your journey to navigate, not theirs. Allow the Universe to manifest its miracles through you.

So, I ask you. What do you desire? What brings you joy? Are you ready to receive?

One day you will think back to this moment and it will provide you with a greater understanding of how much you have grown. It will show the work you have done for yourself and others. You are clearing your path!!

Conclusion

When I started this book I started it with the mindset that if my journey of self-discovery only helped one person and that person was me then it was a success. The truth is I manifested this book. When I wrote my first manifesto I wanted to use my abilities to help others and grow my skill--this book is part of that. When you feel like you do not know how you will get somewhere or how things will happen for you I want you to take a deep breath. After that deep breath I want you to think, "I am right where I need to be." This moment right here is part of what I am here to learn.

What is yours will always be yours and no one can ever take that from you. Even if it is yours for a moment it is still yours. Your passion and your dreams are yours, do not let anyone take them from you, allow them to motivate you and lead you. When you always do things from the heart, they become the purest intentions.

Do not worry about success, fame or even the how. Sometimes when things do not go in our favor we are being led in a different direction. Allow yourself to be flexible and show yourself compassion in those times. Trust that when you put the right intention and are living in true alignment with your heart's desires the universe will continue to show up for you. At first the results may be small, but accept the small wins and be grateful. As you continue to allow your light to shine and fully trust that the universe says, "Yes" and our mind says, "No". You are a limitless being.

You are a part of the universe and the universe is a part of you. Do not turn your back on your wants, needs and desires. Never have regrets and never let your light dim to make someone else comfortable. Allow your light to shine by living a life in alignment with your purpose. You are worthy of all the love and abundance of the universe. Remember it starts with you and the world you see.

I am sure there will come a time of reflection after reading this book. When this happens I want you to go back and ask yourself these questions again, then compare them to your original answers. Did the response change?

1: If we were sitting on the moon together looking down at the earth, what would your world look like to you?

2: Would you be proud of what you see, or would you want to change it?

Works Cited

GODDARD, N. (2013). *THE COMPLETE READER.* AUDIO ENLIGHTENMENT.

JONES, D. R. (2012). *DANCING WITH THE UNIVIERSE A JOURNEY FROM SPIRITUAL RESISTANCE TO SPIRITUAL RELEASE.* ROYAL TREASURES PUBLISHING .

Tolle, E. (2001). *THE POWER OF NOW.* Yogi Immpressions.

Acknowledgments

Thank you to everyone that inspired and supported me while writing this book. There are so many people I could list. I first want to thank the Universe for showing up for me especially when I did not want to show up for myself. I am grateful for the awakening that brought me to realize the more I began to show up for myself the more the Universe would show up for me in return. Only then, did I realize that I truly was part of the Universe and the Universe was a part of me. Thank you to my mom and dad who chose me to be their daughter. The lessons were not always easy, but I would not be where I am now if it were not for you. To my children, thank you for showing me what unconditional love is all about. When I started my journey, I wanted to heal myself. During the journey I realized that by healing myself it would allow me to give you the love you always deserved. Thank you to the people that entered my life even if it was for a moment. Those moments were steps along my path and no matter how small they have influenced my journey in some way shape or form. A big thankful for the friends that have become family along the way.

I am a better version of myself today because of lessons you all have brought along the way. Last but certainly not least, a very special thank you to Braelyn DeRocher for all the time and loving energy he put into believing in my book and my message. Love and Light Always!

About the Author

I am many things. My life is my story. I am a lover, a fighter, a mother, a friend, a writer, and in some people's lives I am a villain. The truth is just like you have played many roles this lifetime. On my journey I have learned that we all have things in our lives that make us, break us and lead us to where we are now. If you want traditional education, I have a master's degree in business administration from Central Michigan University with a concentration of human resources. I have continuing education certifications that would take up the whole page of this blog. If you are anything like me or even relate to me, you probably spent a lifetime chasing a dream just to discover that dream was not your true heart's desire at all. I am a medium. You are probably thinking the same thing I did when I started discovering my gifts. You can talk to spirits? The answer is, yes, but it is more than that--It is all about energy. I am also trained in Chakra energy cleansing, EFT tapping, mindfulness, numerology, mediumship, master tarot and intuition training courses. I am a firm believer that there is always more knowledge to be found so I am constantly reading, listening to podcasts, mediating and being a conscientious observer to develop my gift. My soul purpose is to use my gifts to lift others up and live my most authentic life. I desire to lead others to live the life of abundance they desire. I believe that all souls are here to fulfill their own divine purpose. I wholeheartedly believe that love is the key to restoring humanity. It is my belief that a person can only love another person as much as they love themselves. I value teaching others to believe in themselves, love themselves unconditionally and meet others with acceptance just as they are. Guiding others along their spiritual journey is my passion; I love it, I live it, I breathe it. Having the ability to connect with souls on such an intimate level is so humbling. Did I ever imagine I would be leading and assisting others spiritually, professionally and personally navigate their life? No, not at all! I would not change it for anything. I honestly believe it all starts with a conversation between you and me and the world you see.

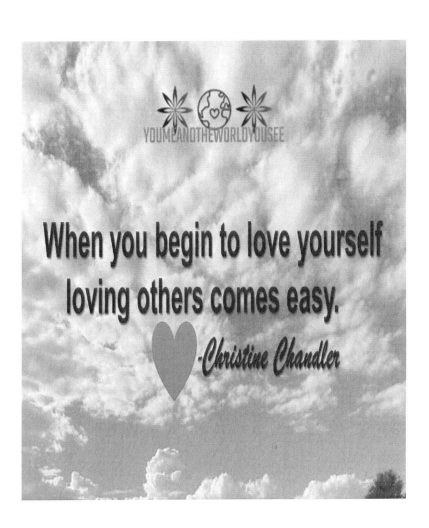

When you begin to love yourself loving others comes easy.

-Christine Chandler

Made in United States
North Haven, CT
19 January 2025

64641740R00067